A Sunshine Garden Doll Pattern

Daisy

By Anne Cote

Daisy

Daisy

**For more Sunshine Garden Dolls Patterns
Visit bluedaisyzone.com**

Sunflower

Poppy　Dandelion　Marigold　Rosemary　Sage　Primrose

ISBN-13: 978-1-940354-61-3

Text, Photos, and Illustrations by Anne Cote
Cover Design by Anne Cote & Layne Walker
Edited by Joan Cote and Layne Walker

First edition published in August 2020
Published by New Friends Publishing, LLC
Lake Havasu City, AZ

Visit New Friends Publishing's Website at
www.newfriendspublishing.com

CONTENTS

To my best friend and love,

Layne Walker,

who holds my hand as we dance through

fields of daisies

Materials for Daisy

Daisy dances to the rhythm of the wind in the garden. She is 20" tall. She has bright blue eyes, dark hair, rosy cheeks and a sunny smile that will warm anyone's heart.

SUPPLIES

There are lots of options for materials, including scraps of fabric and fancy trims. I've listed the products I use in brackets. Other options abound and are listed below.

DOLL

44"x13" cotton fabric for body [Lightweight Muslim]
Craft paint, markers, pastel stick
　　　[Anita's Navy Blue for eyes; Anita's White for dots in the eyes]
　　　[Sharpie Permanent Markers for nose, brows, lashes, mouth]
　　　[Rosy red pastel stick for cheeks]
Yarn for hair [Yarn Bee Fireside "Honey Maple"]
Poly-fil Stuffing 6-8 oz.
Stuffing tools [tube and stick]
Fabric turning tools [tube and stick, see instructions]

CLOTHING

44"x19" cotton floral fabric for bloomers, top, and skirt
31x17" contrasting cotton fabric for pinafore
32"x5" cotton fabric for hair bows
12"x8" black felt for shoes

30" 1/2"-1" lace trim (flat or gathered) for skirt
18" 1/2"-1" lace trim (flat or gathered) for bloomers
11" 1/2"-1" lace trim (flat or gathered) for neckline
11" 1/2"-1" lace trim (flat or gathered) for sleeves
　　　(Total trim: 70")
34" rickrack for pinafore trim

18" 1/4" elastic for bloomers and skirt
3 snap fasteners
2 buttons for decoration on straps of pinafore
General sewing supplies

OPTIONS

Face can be painted, embroidered, or drawn on with permanent markers.
Cheek blush can be made with powdered blush or chalks.
Bloomers in a contrasting color takes 20"x10" of fabric.
Top in contrasting color takes 26"x7" of fabric.
Skirt in contrasting color takes 32"x11" of fabric.
Hair instructions are for hand sewing. Glue can be used instead, or a combination of sewing and glue.
Hair Bow can be made with bias tape or ribbon, rather than cut and sewn.
Trim can be flat or gathered. A flat trim can replace the rickrack on the pinafore.
Snaps can be plastic or metal or replaced by buttons.

COPYRIGHT and CHILD SAFETY

COPYRIGHT

What *CAN* you do? You *CAN* sell the items that you make from this pattern. You can use the templates to create the doll. You can also add your own artistic flare to what you create when using the templates. What you make is your property and is yours to do with as you wish.

What *CAN'T* you do? You *CANNOT* copy the pattern illustrations, diagrams, written instructions or photos. You cannot simply photocopy, scan, or reproduce the sewing pattern in any way and then sell copies of it. This is an infringement of copyright laws.

CHILD SAFETY

This doll is advised for children 3 years or older. For a younger child or baby, bows, sashes, ribbons, or any loose parts should be removed or sewn securely onto the doll or clothing. Fancy laces can wear out with use and separate from the clothing. They are preferable for children over 3. Plastic baby snaps can be used instead of metal snaps. The pattern calls for painting the face. Embroidery and painting are safety measures. Buttons should not be used for eyes for small children. I cannot be responsible for the way each crafter uses these patterns or instructions. Please consider the age of the child for which you are making the doll.

For more information on copyright laws and safety information, there is a great amount of information on the internet. For pattern questions, please send an email to Anne at this address: bluedaisyzone@gmail.com

Website: bluedaisyzone.com

Making the Doll

All seam allowances are 1/4 inch.

Use a small machine stich for more stability.

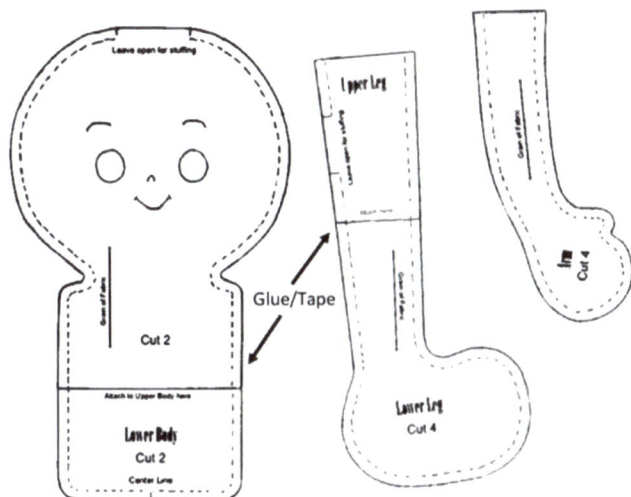

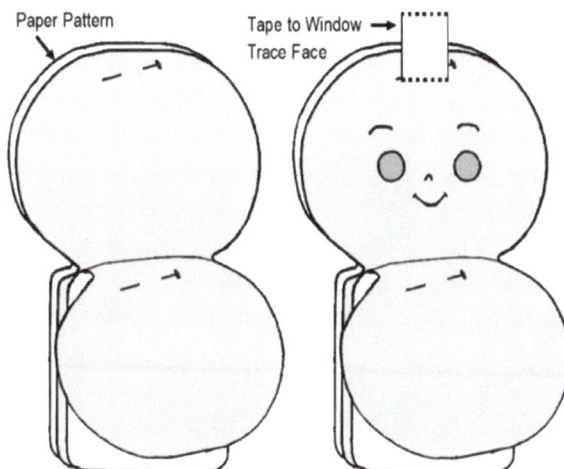

Cut out the patterns. Glue or tape the leg and body pieces together where indicated. Pin to fabric and cut out pieces.

FACE: Lay the fabric head/body on top of the paper pattern. Pin one side of the fabric head to the pattern top. Pin the folded layer of fabric to the lower body. Tape or hold the head/body to a window or lightbox and trace the face with pencil.

All the features can be painted or embroidered. I use acrylic paint for the eyes and Sharpie Permanent Markers for the nose, mouth, brows, and eyelashes. Don't forget to add a white dot to the eyes.

Daisy's eyes are blue. The lashes are black. The brows are brown. The nose and mouth are red. A reddish-pink powdered blush or pastel stick for her cheeks works well with her blue eyes and dark hair.

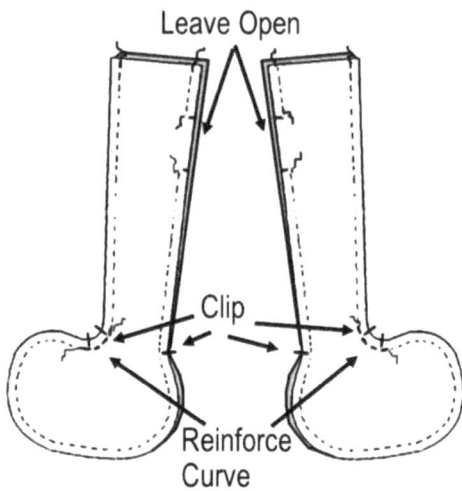

LEGS: Right sides together, stitch the legs, leaving the opening in the upper section for stuffing. Reinforce the curve between the top of the foot and leg. Clip curves.

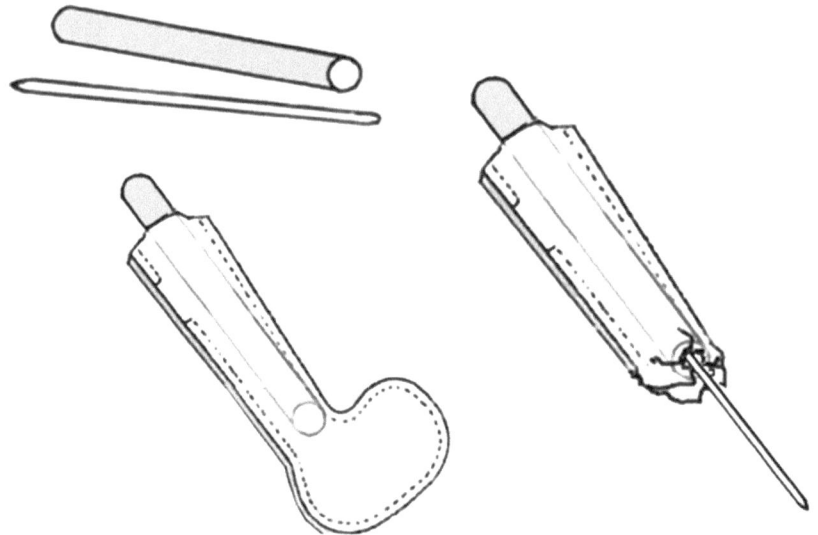

Turn the legs right side out. My favorite way of turning narrow fabric pieces is with a tube and stick. In this case, push the tube inside the leg. With the stick, push the foot into the tube until it comes out the other end.

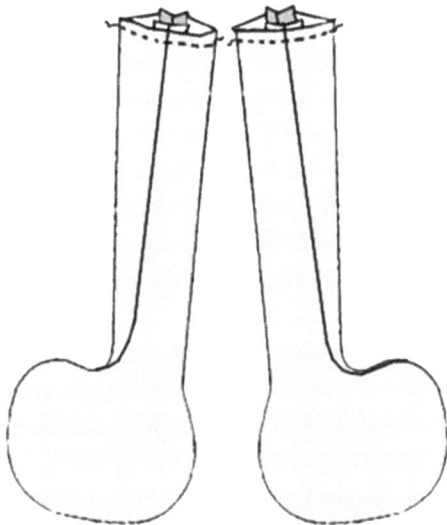

Open the top of the legs and pin the seams together. Baste across the top.

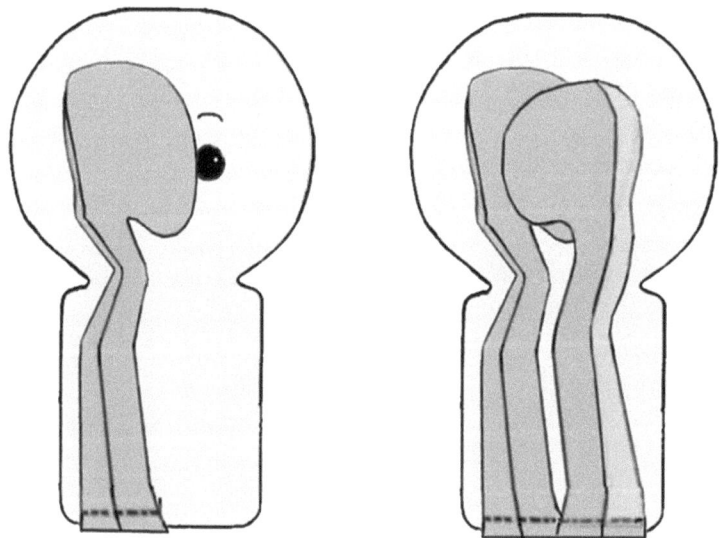

Place the top of the legs on the bottom of the right side of the body with the face. It's very important that the toes face the features on the face. Otherwise, the feet and legs will come out backwards. The leg tops should lie 1/4 inch from the side of the body on both sides. The legs should hang just below the body about 1/8 inch to make sure they are caught in the stitches. The legs might overlap a little in the middle. Pin/baste the legs in place along the bottom of the body.

4

Leave Open

Clip

Reinforce Neck Curve

Ladder Stitch

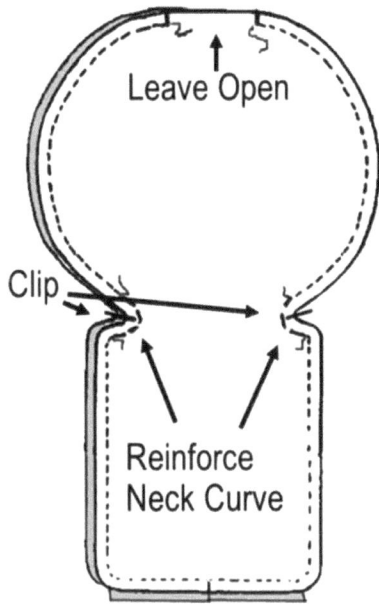

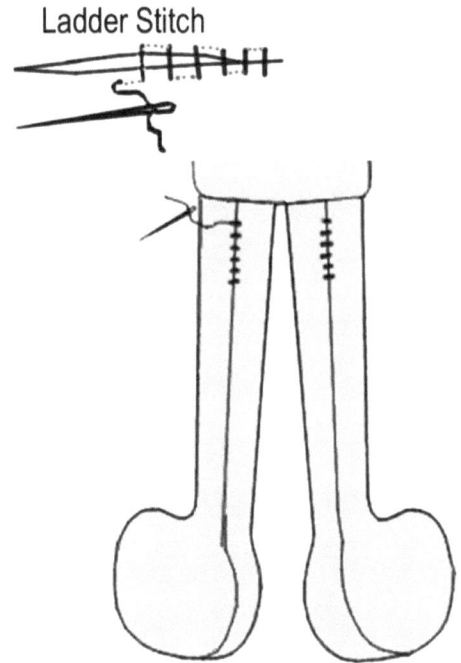

BODY: Right sides together, pin/baste the entire body, making sure the feet and legs are not caught in the seam allowance. Starting at the head, stitch around the entire body, leaving the opening for the stuffing. Reinforce the neck area with extra stitches. Clip the curves.

Turn the body right side out. Stuff the body and head. Sew the head closed with a ladder stitch as shown above.

On the back side, stuff the legs. Close the legs with a ladder stitch.

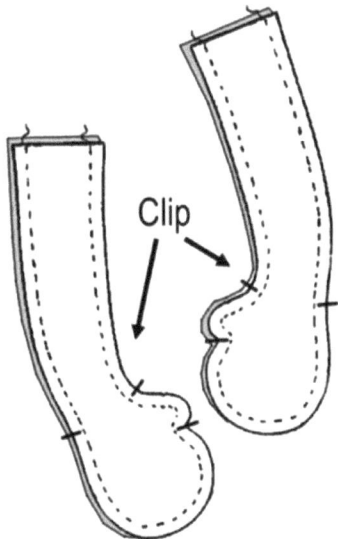

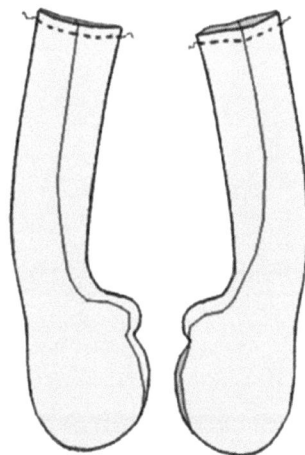

Overcast Stitch

Clip

ARMS: Right sides together, stitch the arms. Clip curves. Turn right side out.

Stuff the arms to about 1 inch from the top. Turn the top edge inside 1/4 inch and pin closed. Hand sew or machine stitch closed.

Pin arms to shoulders. Stitch by hand with an overcast stitch.

Making the Hair

Please read all the instructions before starting the hair.

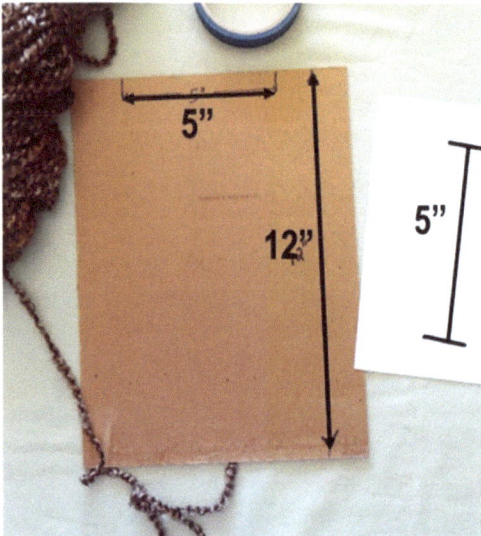

1. Preparation: On a piece of copy paper (or material stabilizer) draw a 5-inch line down the middle. Use a piece of cardboard that measures 12 inches on one side and at least 5 inches on the other side.

2. Wrap the yarn around the 12-inch side of the cardboard 70 times. Place a piece of masking tape about 1 inch down from the top of the yarn on both sides of the cardboard. This holds the yarn strands together for sewing. Cut the yarn at the opposite end of the tape.

3. Carefully move the yarn from the cardboard and center it across the 5-inch line on the paper. The tape should hold it in place on both sides of the paper.

4. Machine stitch the yarn down the middle between the tape pieces. Use a small stitch to create more perforations, which will make the paper easier to remove. Remove the tape and the paper.

5. Using string or yarn, loosely tie the yarn together on both ends about four inches from the end. This will help make it easier to handle when attaching to the doll's head.

6. BANGS: Use a piece of cardboard that is 3 inches wide and at least 5½ inches long. Prepare a piece of copy paper with a line 5½ inches long.

7. Wrap yarn 45 times around the 3-inch side of the cardboard, covering 5 1/2 inches across the top. Place tape about 1/2 inch from the top of the cardboard on both sides. Cut the bottom of the yarn. Center the tape on each side of the line on the copy paper. Stitch with a small stitch. Remove the tape and paper.

8. Center the seam of the larger section of hair on the doll's forehead about 1/4 inch in front of the fabric seam line. Pin in place. On the back of the head, line up the part between the forehead and neck. Pin in place. Using an overstitch with a thread matching the yarn, sew the yarn to the doll's head from the neck to the forehead.

9. Center the open seam line of the bangs on the top of the doll's head. Place the seam line just in front of the hair line. Using an overstitch, sew the bangs to the doll's head.

NOTE: To create pigtails on top of the head, the yarn must be tacked to the center back of the head down the part and to the side of the head. This is my method.

Lay Towel over Right Side

Separate Yarn Near Part

Stitch Yarn to Side of Head

10. Separate the yarn on the back of the head to each side. Lay a towel over the right side of the yarn while working on the left side. Separate about 1/3 of the strands of hair on the left side and lay them over the towel.

11. Using an overstitch, sew the strands from the neck up and around the side of the face to the top of the head. Stitch along the head's seam line.

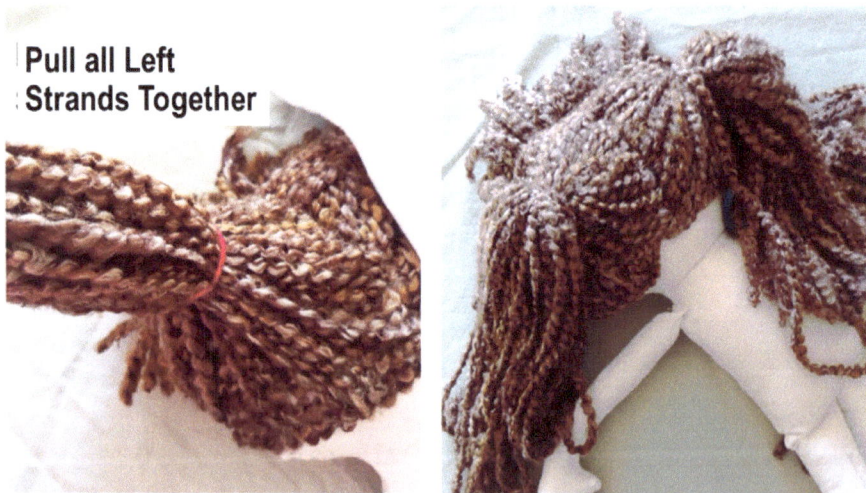

Pull all Left Strands Together

12. Join all the strands on the left side. Pull them up toward the top of the head. Tie them together with a rubber band, hair band, or piece of yarn.

13. Repeat #10 through #12 for the right side of the head. Trim pigtails and bangs as desired.

Making the Clothes

All seam allowances are 1/4 inch.

Cut out paper pattern pieces and glue/tape Skirt Front to Skirt Back. Cut out fabric.

All edges can be finished by using an overstitch or making a tiny fold inward on the edge of the fabric. I use a pinking shears to cut out my pattern pieces and leave this as my finished edge.

Bloomers

Fold up lower edge of bloomers 1/4 inch. Press.

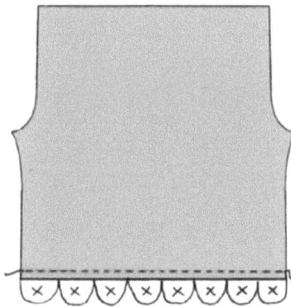

Pin/baste trim to lower edge and stitch. You can attach the trim on either side of the fabric, depending on your preference or on the finished edge of the trim.

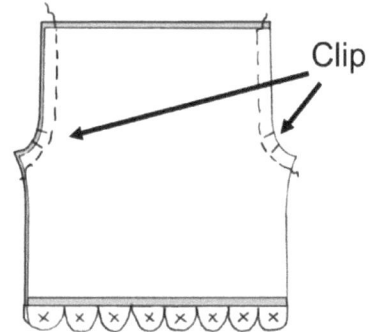

Clip

With right sides together, stitch the crotch seams. Clip curves.

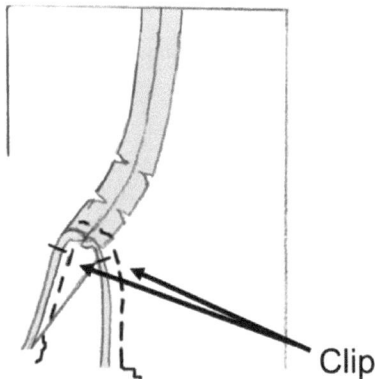

Leave open

Insert Elastic on Safety Pin

Stitch closed

Clip

Right sides together, stitch leg seams from crotch to trim on both sides. Clip curves near crotch. Press seam

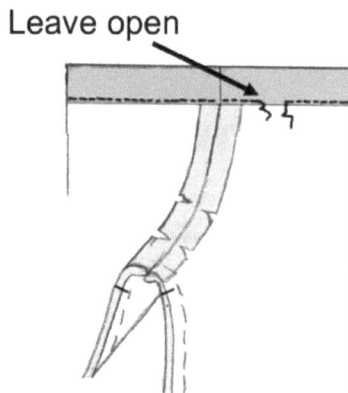

Fold top edge over 1/4 inch then another 1/2 inch to form casing for elastic. Press. Stitch near lower edge. Leave a section open for inserting elastic.

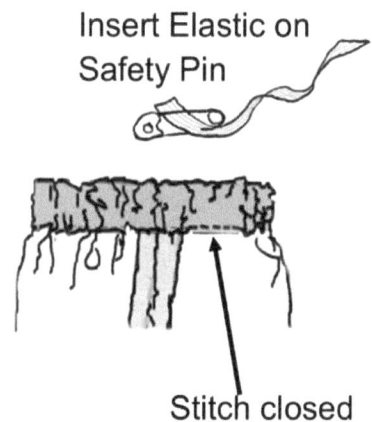

Cut 9 inches of elastic. Insert into the casing on a safety pin. Push pin through to the other side. Overlap the elastic 1/4 inch. Stitch elastic together securely by hand. By hand or machine, stitch the casing closed.

Clip

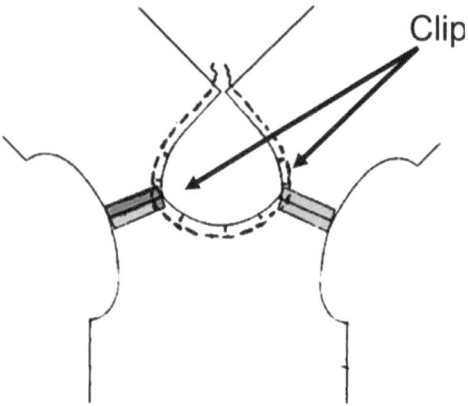

Right bodice sides together, stitch shoulder seams. Press seams open. Stay-stitch around neck to give it stability. Clip curves.

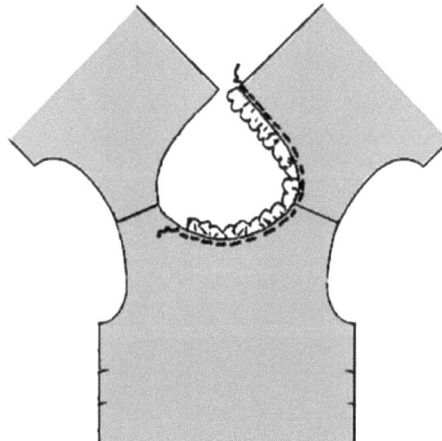

Press neck edge under at stay-stitching. Pin/baste trim to neck and stitch. Trim can be sewn on inside or outside of fabric, depending on preference or on the finished edge of the trim.

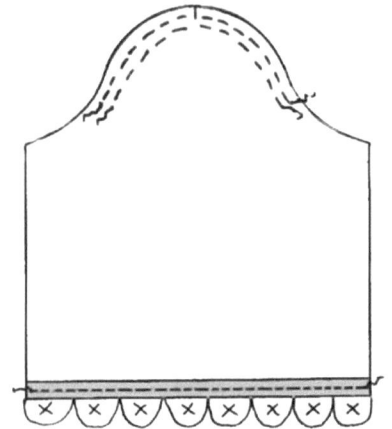

Make two rows of a running stitch at the top of the sleeve for gathering. Press the lower edge under 1/4 inch. Pin/baste trim and stitch.

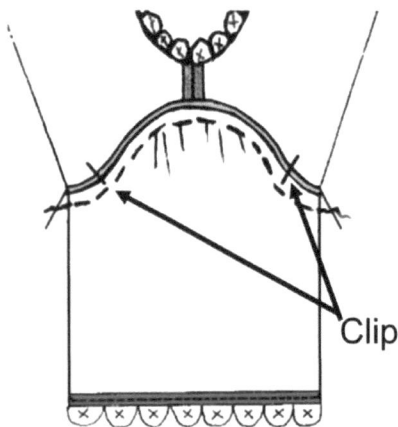

Clip

Right sides together, match center of sleeve to the shoulder seam. Pull up gathering threads to fit armhole. Pin/baste sleeve to armhole and stitch. Clip curves.

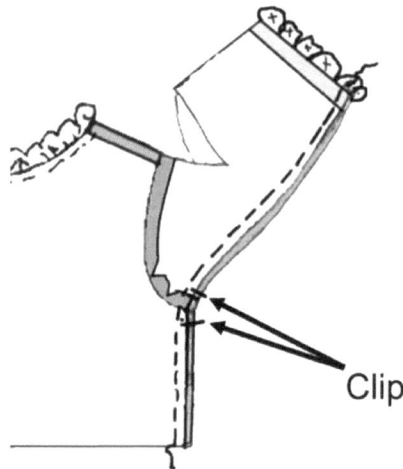

Clip

Fold armhole seam toward sleeve. Pin/baste and stitch the underarm seams from the bodice to the end of the sleeve trim. Clip curves where bodice and sleeve meet.

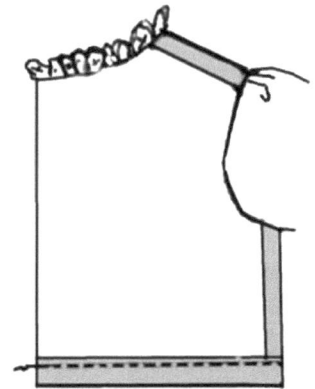

Press lower edge under 1/4 inch, then another 1/4 inch to form hem. Stitch.

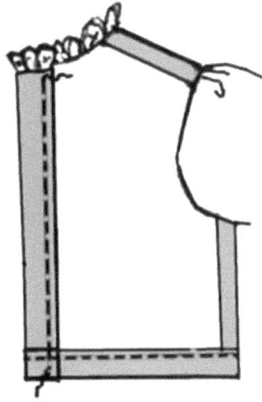

Fold facing over wrong side of bodice. Press and stitch.

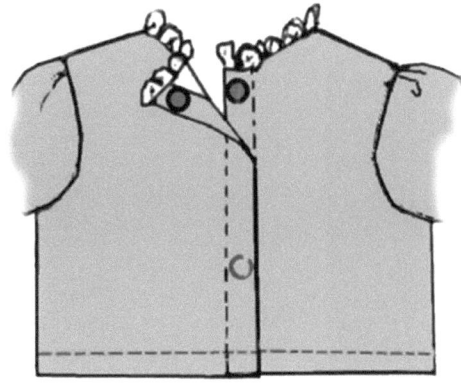

Overlap the left side on top of the right side. Attach snaps to top of bodice and below middle of bodice.

Skirt

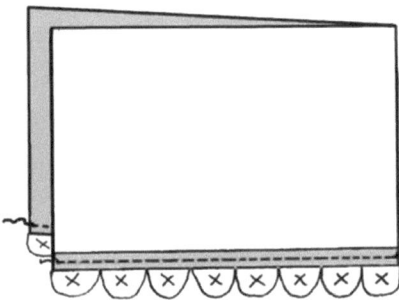

Fold bottom edge under 1/4 inch. Press. Pin/baste trim and stitch.

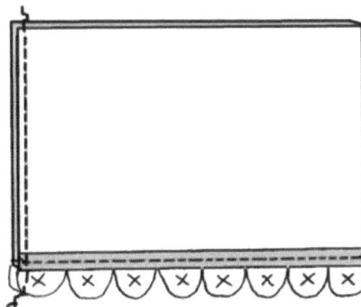

Right sides together, pin and stitch back seam.

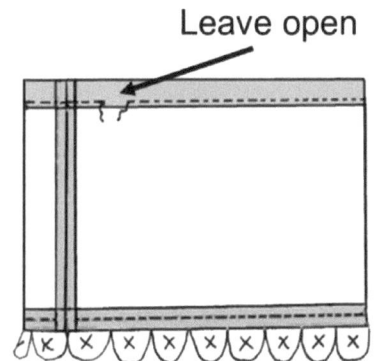

Leave open

Fold top edge over 1/4 inch, then another 1/2 inch to form casing for elastic. Press and stitch near lower edge. Leave a section open to insert the elastic.

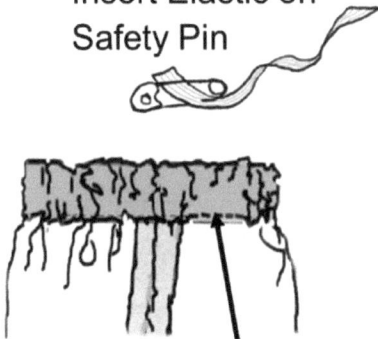

Insert Elastic on Safety Pin

Stitch closed

Cut 9 inches of elastic. Insert into the casing on a safety pin. Push pin through to the other side. Overlap the elastic 1/4 inch and stitch elastic together securely. By hand or machine, stitch the casing closed.

Pinafore

Daisy Pinafore Front

Daisy Pinafore Back

Cut 2

Back

Front

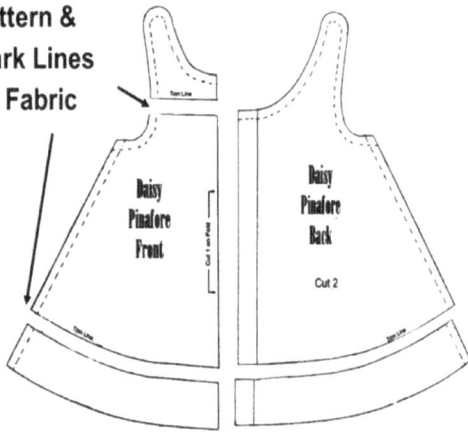

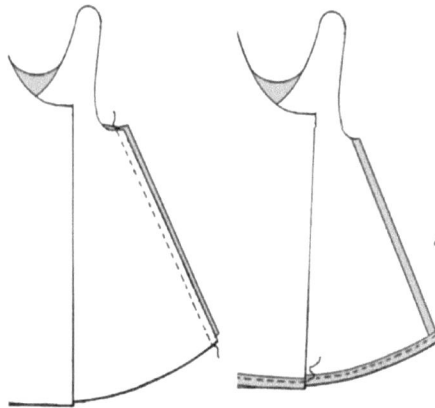

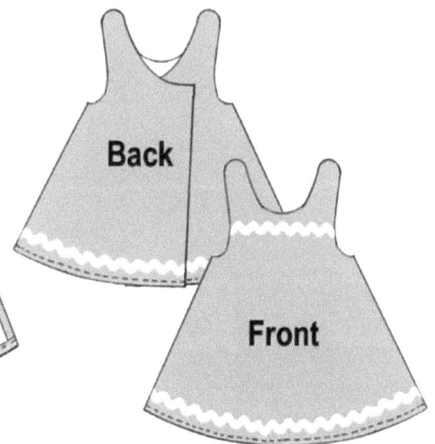

Option1: To mark trim lines on fabric, cut the paper pattern at trim lines, lay on fabric, and draw the lines with pencil. (See above.)

Option 2: Place pattern and fabric on window and trace lines.

Option 3: Use fabric tracing paper.

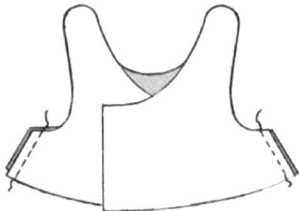

Right sides together, sew pinafore side seams. Press seams open. Press hem up 1/4 inch then another 1/4 inch. Pin and stitch.

Pin/baste trim on fabric trim lines and stitch in place.

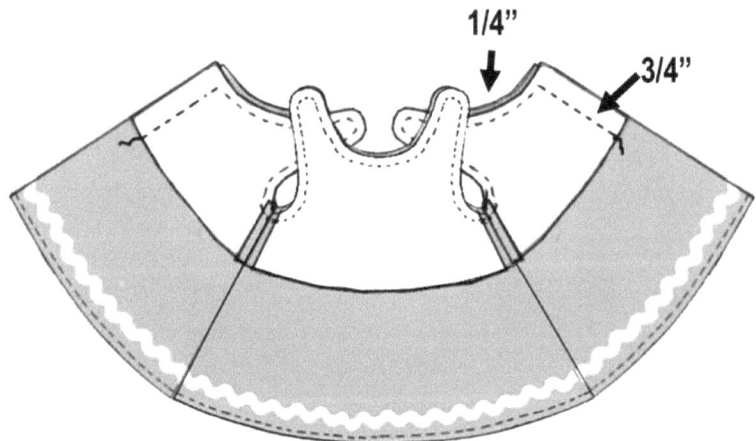

1/4"   3/4"

With right sides of facing together, pin and stitch side seams. Finish lower edge as desired.

Right sides together, pin/baste facing to pinafore. On the back facing edges, stitch 3/4 inch in from the raw edge.

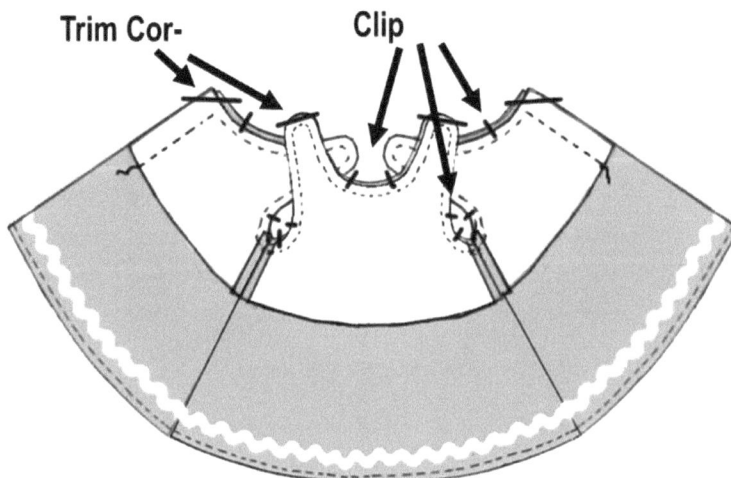

Trim Cor-   Clip

Clip curves and trim corners. Turn right side out and press. Facing on lower part of pinafore should press toward the wrong side 3/4 inch.

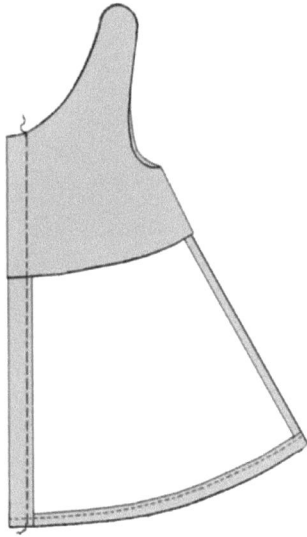

Stich the facing close to raw edge on both sides of the back.

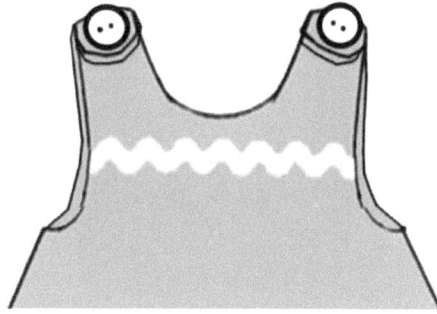

Loop the back strap over the front strap and attach a button for decoration. There is no button hole.

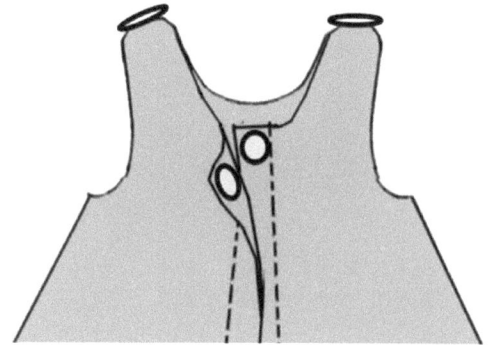

On the back, make sure the left side is on top of the right side. Attach one snap at the top.

Hair Bows

Leave Open

Clip Corners

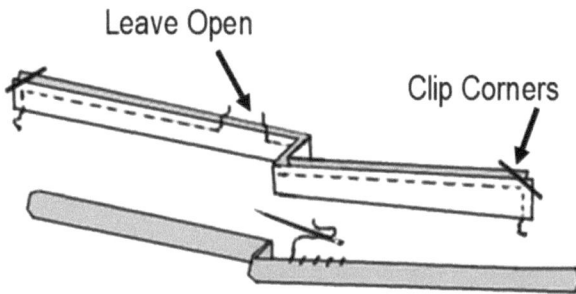

For hair bows, cut two pieces of fabric 32"x2½". Fold the fabric in half longwise. Pin and stitch, starting from each end and leaving about a 1-inch opening near the middle. Clip corners and turn right side out. Close the open section with an overcast stitch.

Shoes

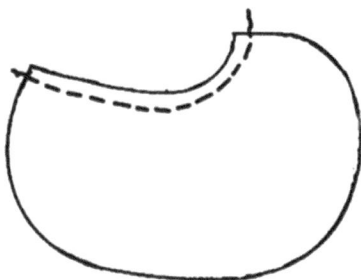

On each shoe piece, stay-stitch along top edge for stability.

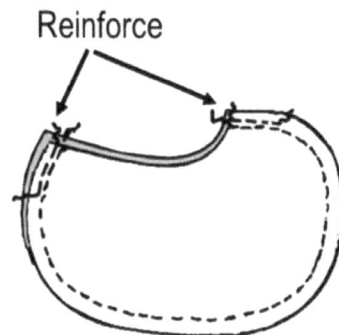

Reinforce

With right sides together, stitch from toe to back of heel. Reinforce beginning and ending with extra stitches for stability.

Patterns
For
Doll and Clothing

Patterns can be cut out or traced.

Leave open for stuffing

Grain of Fabric

Daisy

Cut 2

Attach to Lower Body here

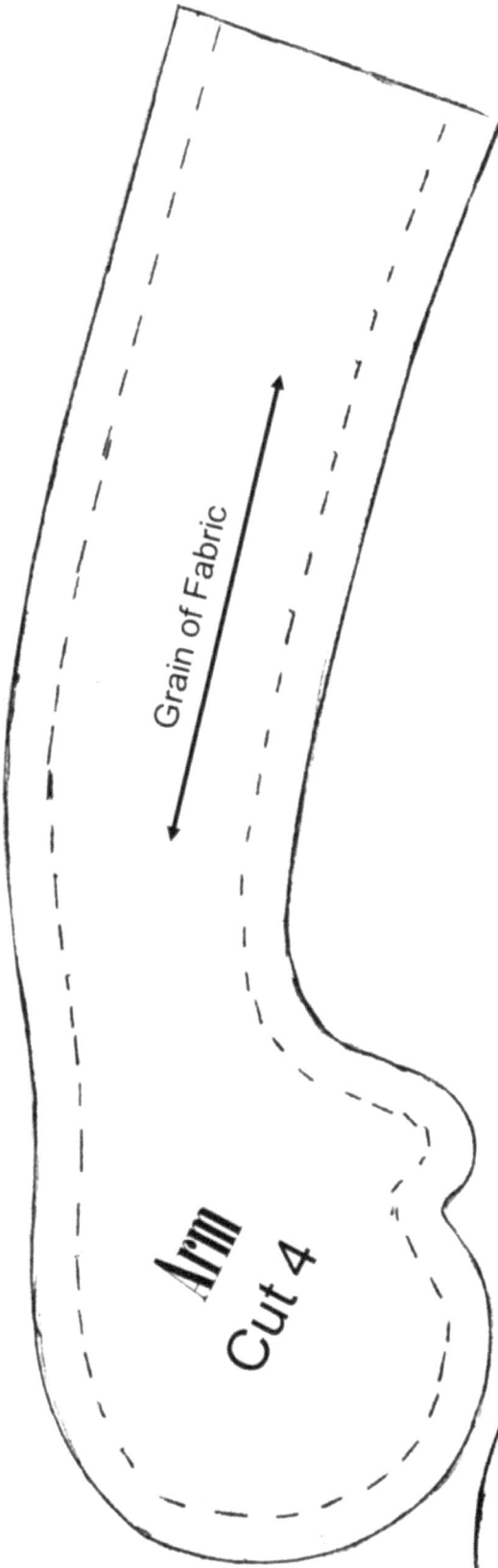

Grain of Fabric

Arm
Cut 4

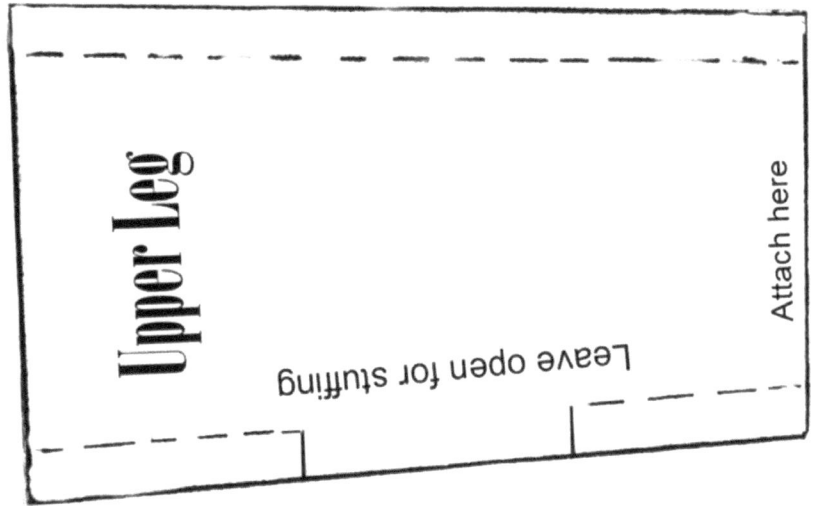

Upper Leg

Attach here

Leave open for stuffing

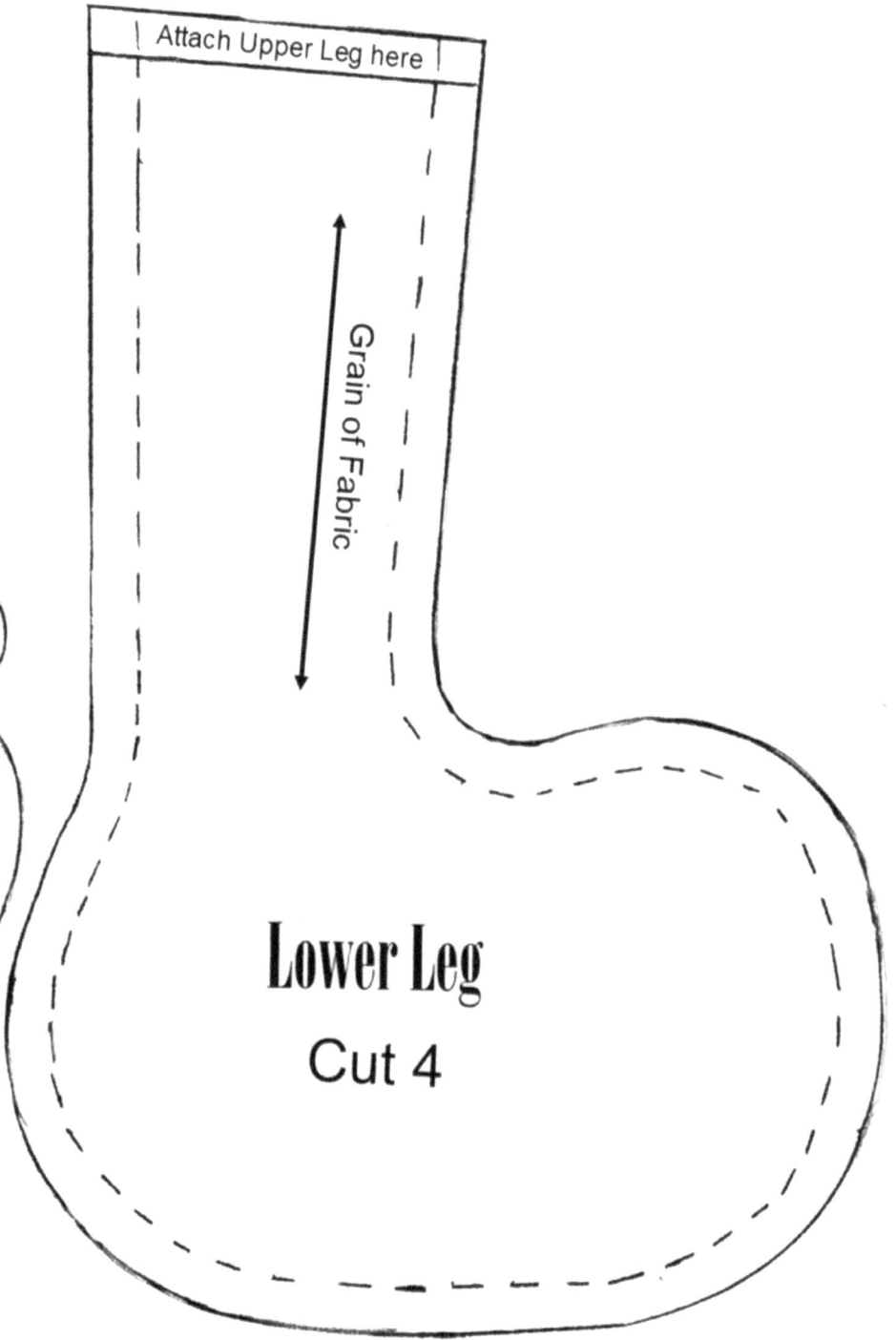

Attach Upper Leg here

Grain of Fabric

Lower Leg

Cut 4

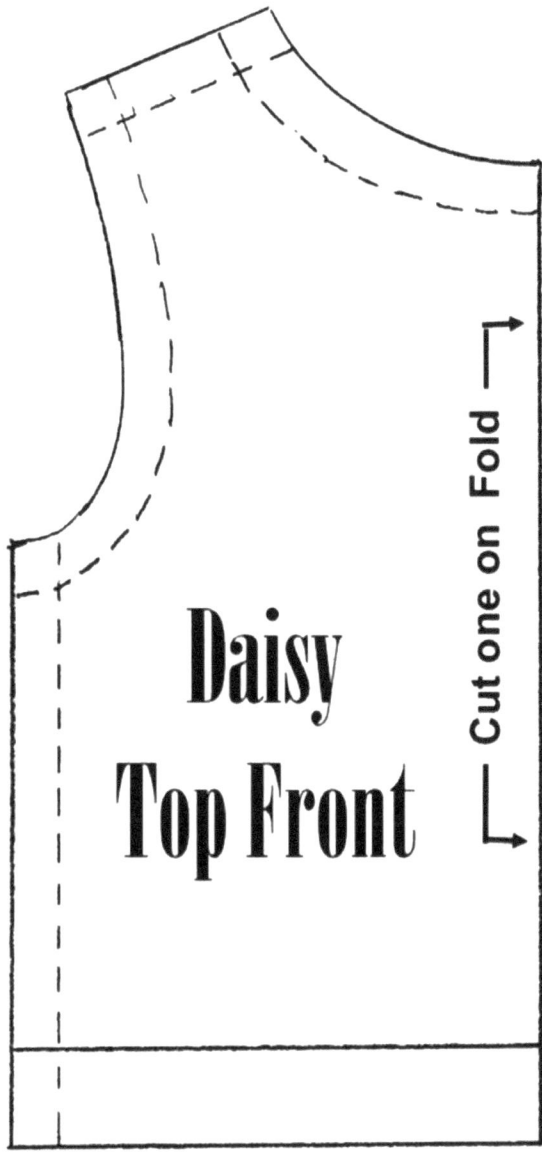

Daisy Top Front

Cut one on Fold

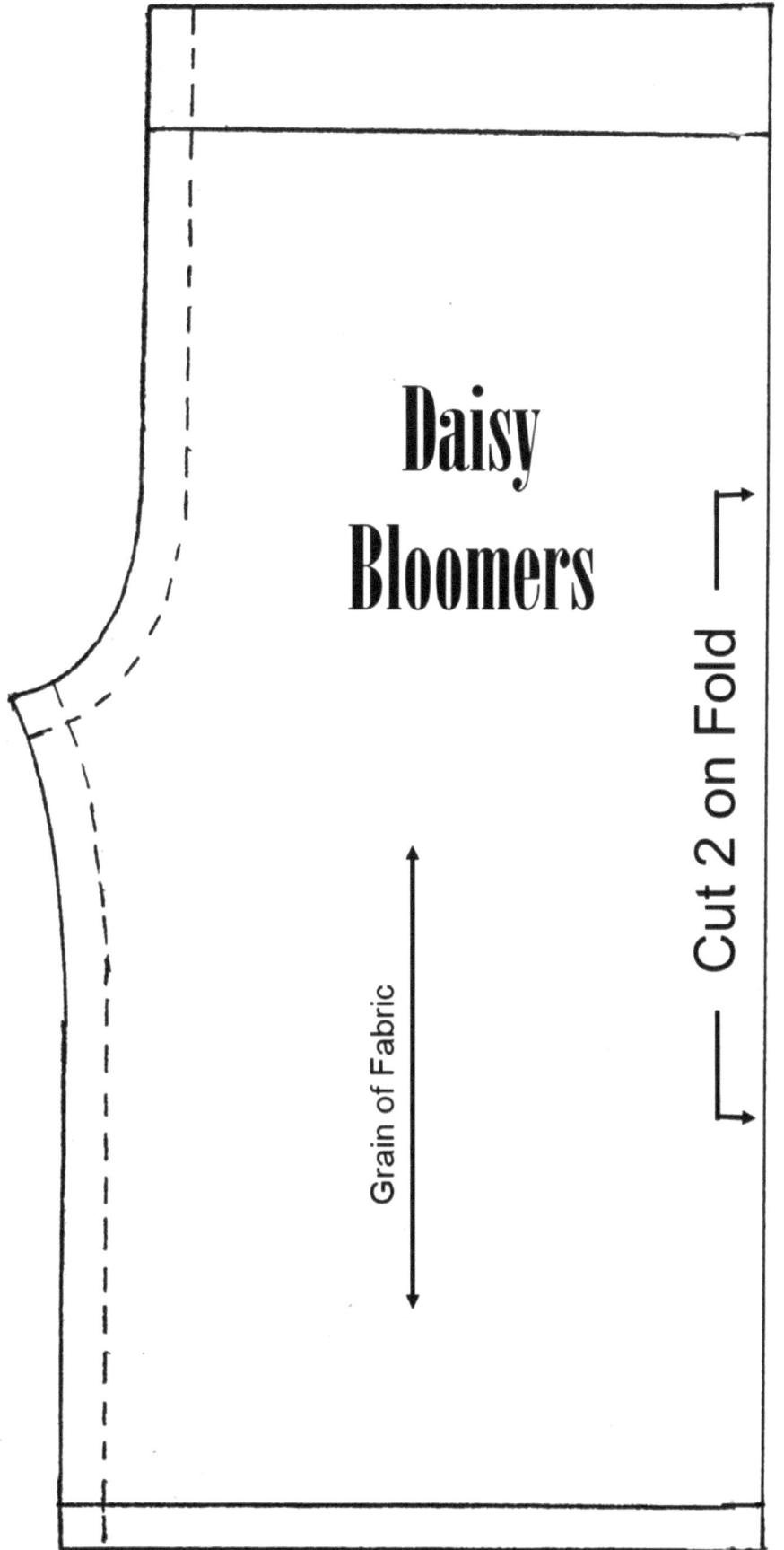

Daisy Bloomers

Grain of Fabric

Cut 2 on Fold

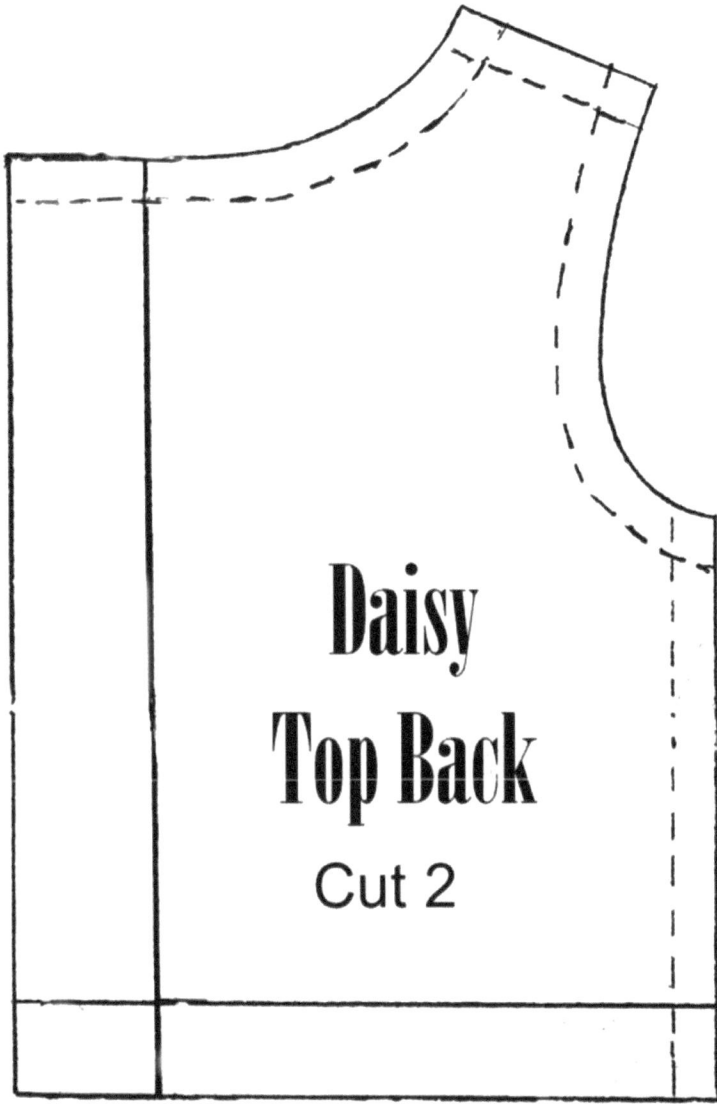

Daisy

Top Back

Cut 2

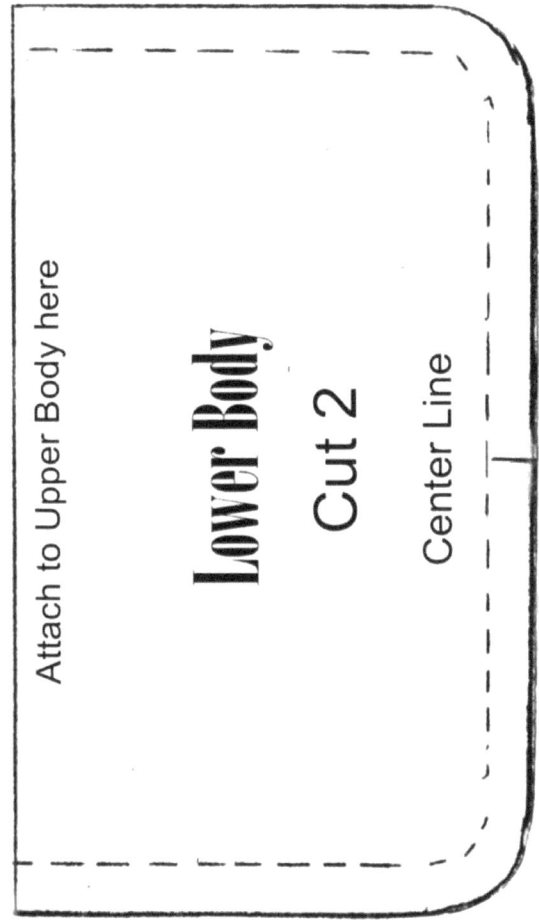

Attach to Upper Body here

Lower Body

Cut 2

Center Line

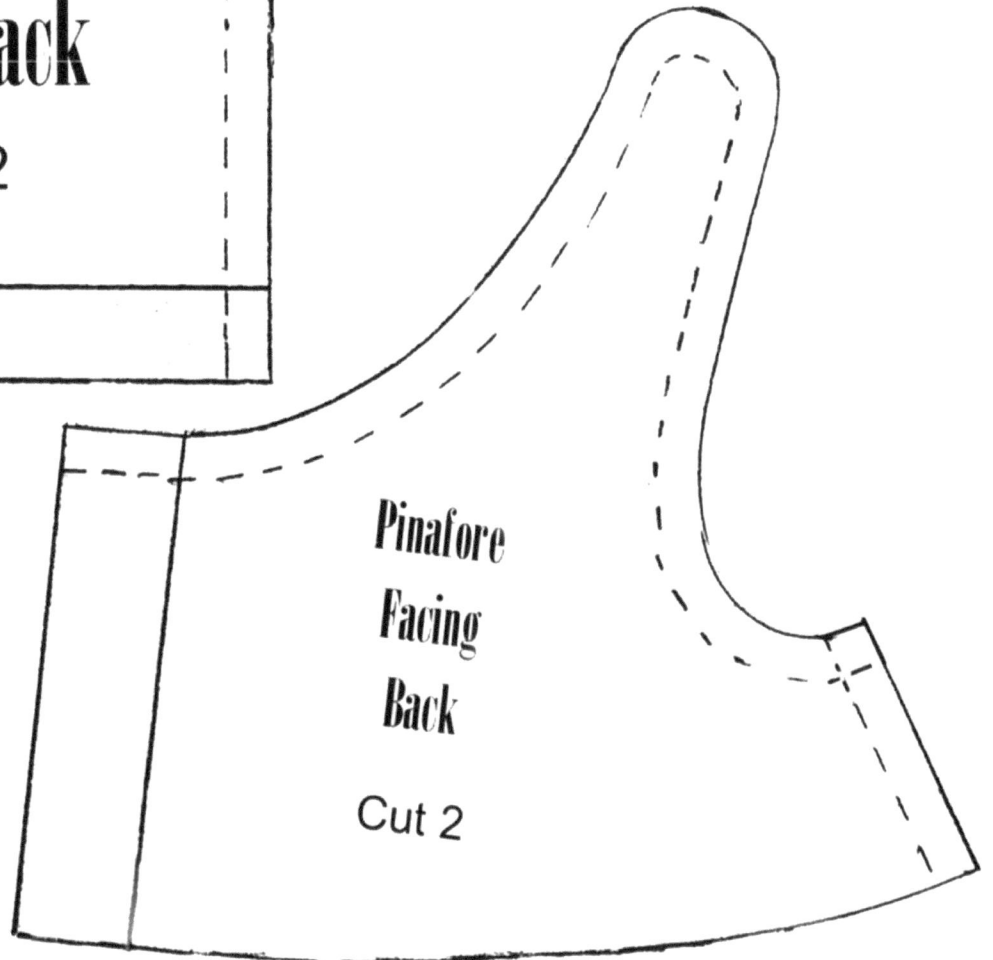

Pinafore

Facing

Back

Cut 2

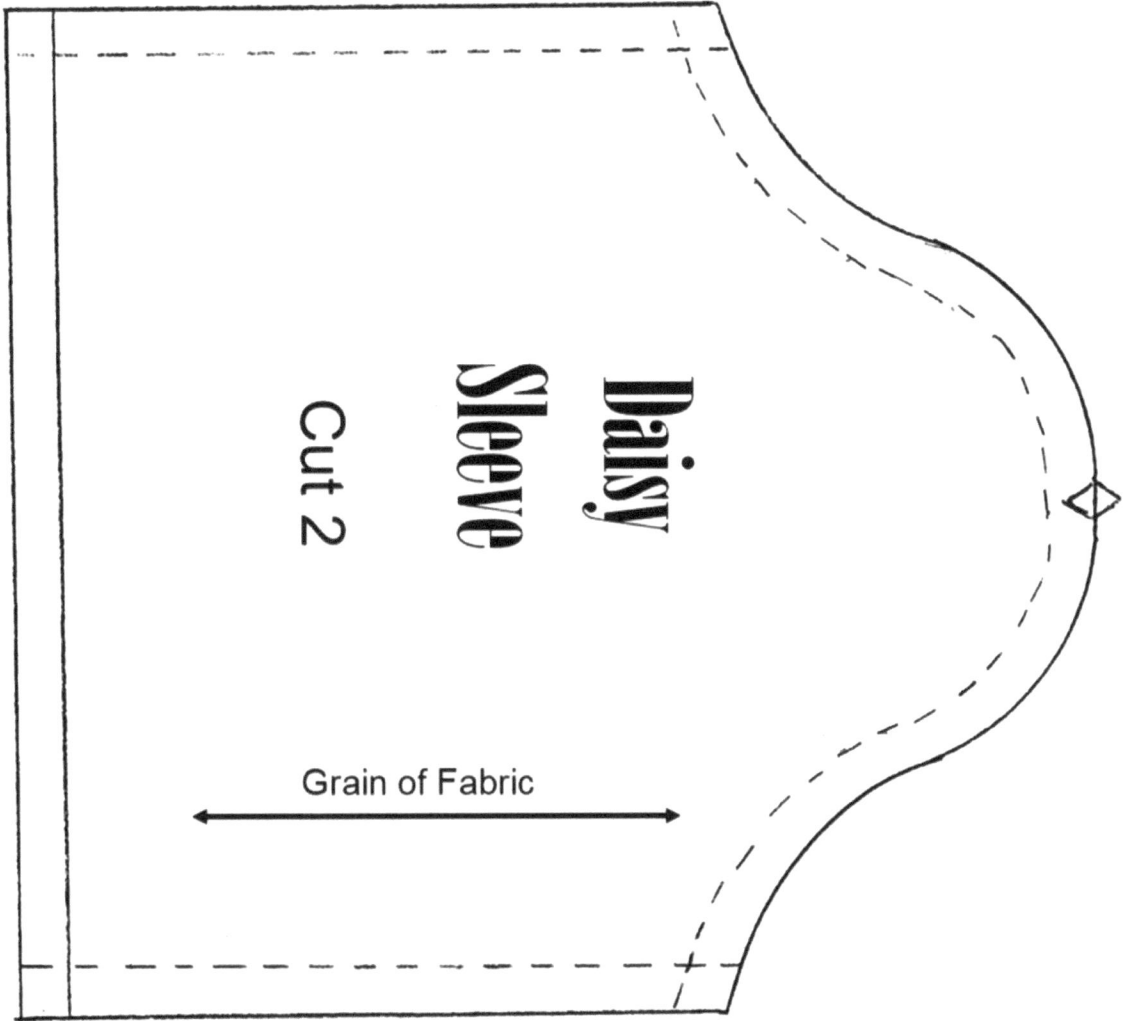

Daisy Sleeve

Cut 2

Grain of Fabric

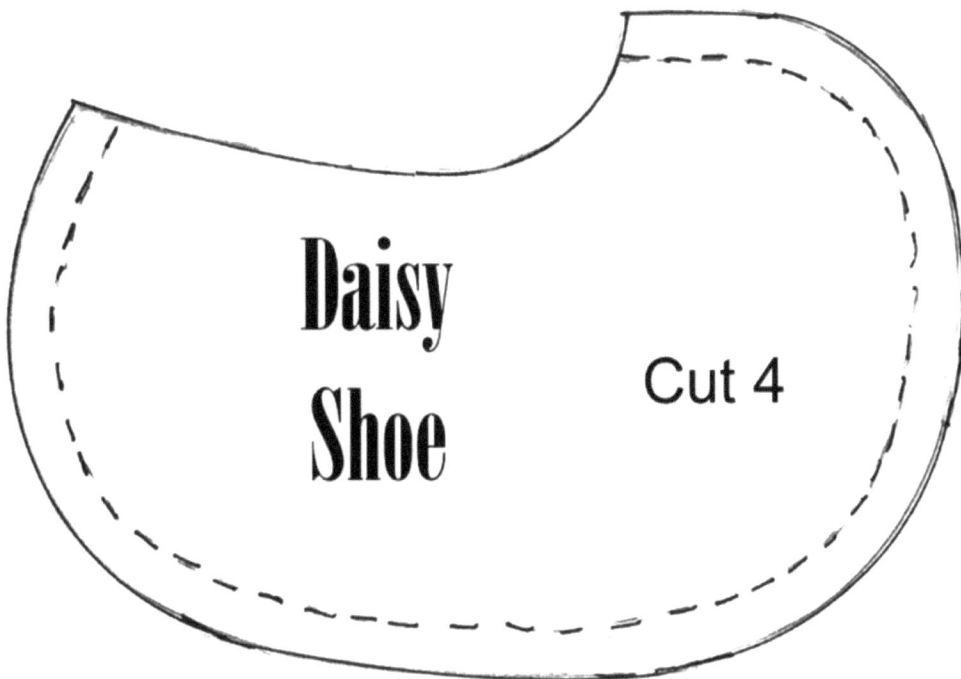

Daisy Shoe

Cut 4

Fold for Casing for Waist Elastic

Daisy
Skirt Front

Attach to Skirt Back here

Cut 1 on Fold

Add Trim here

Back Seam

Daisy
Skirt Back

Attach to Skirt Front here

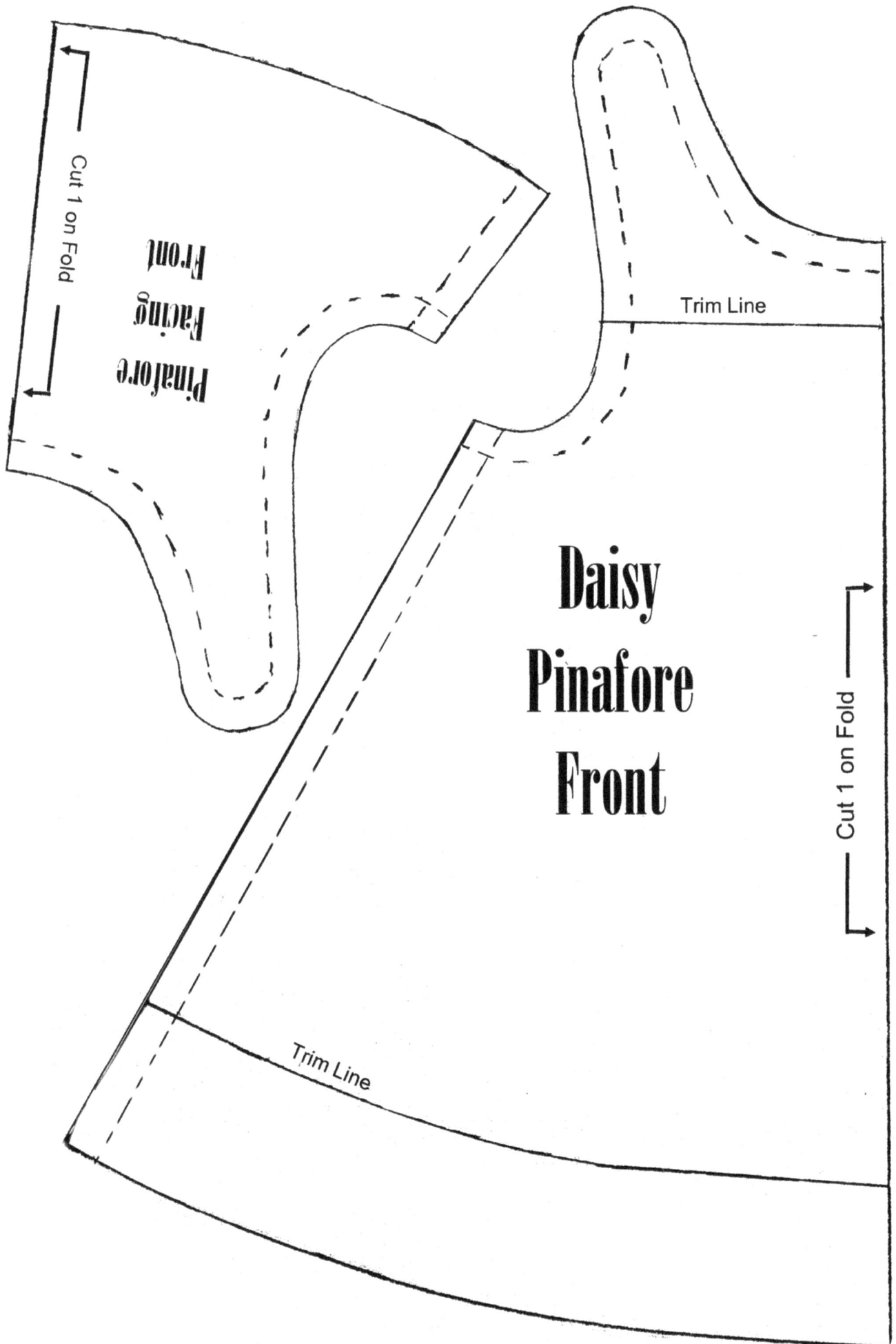

Cut 1 on Fold

Pinafore Facing Front

Daisy Pinafore Front

Trim Line

Cut 1 on Fold

Trim Line

Daisy
Pinafore
Back

Cut 2

Trim Line

www.ingramcontent.com/pod-product-compliance
Lightning Source LLC
Chambersburg PA
CBHW041550040426

42447CB00002B/117